PAT METHENY UNITY GROUP KIN

ISBN 978-1-4803-7103-3

HAL•LEONARD®
CORPORATION
7777 W. BLUEMOUND RD. P.O. BOX 13819 MILWAUKEE, WI 53213

Visit Hal Leonard Online at
www.halleonard.com

On Day One
By Pat Metheny

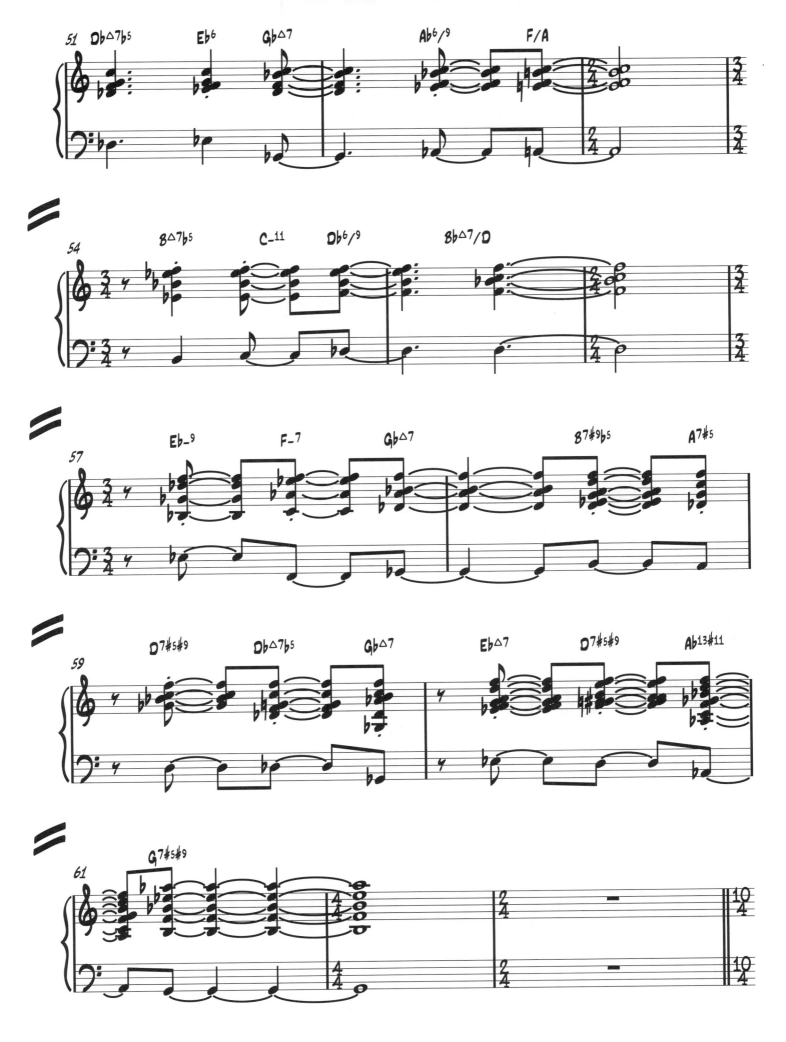

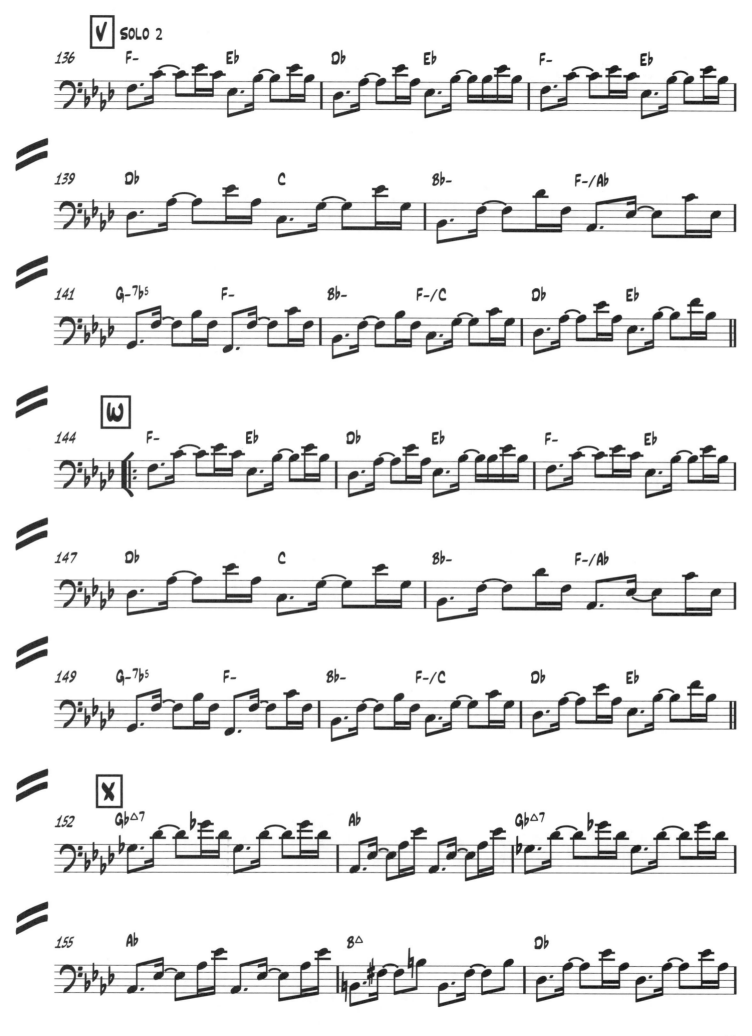

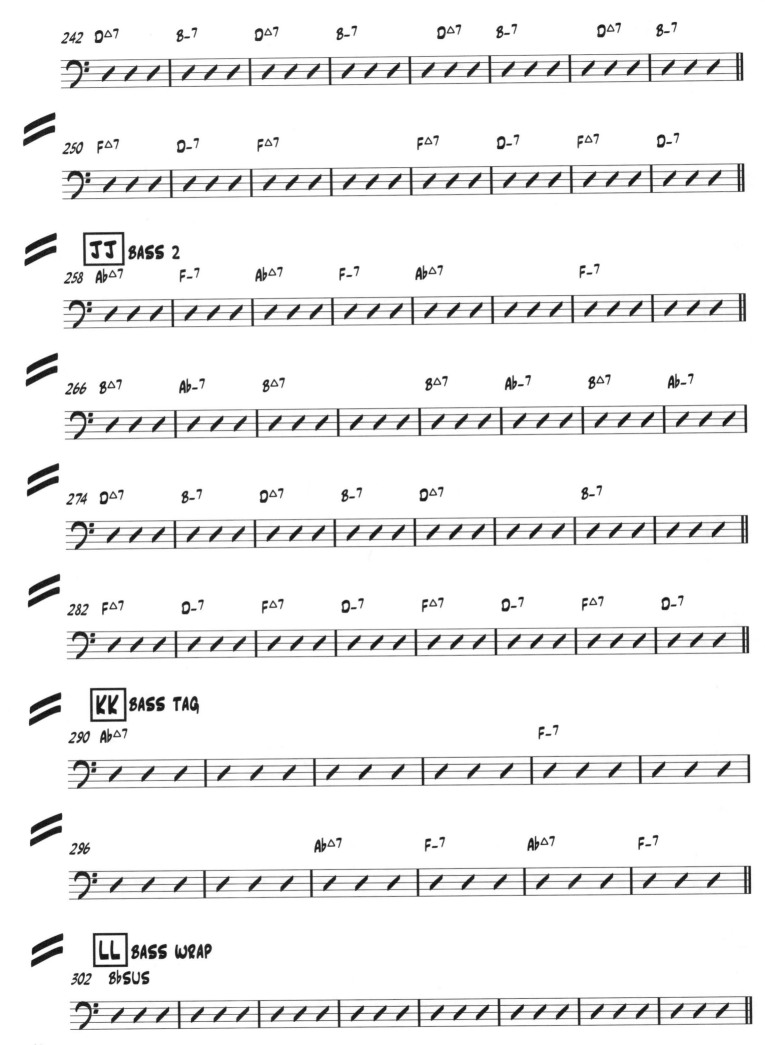

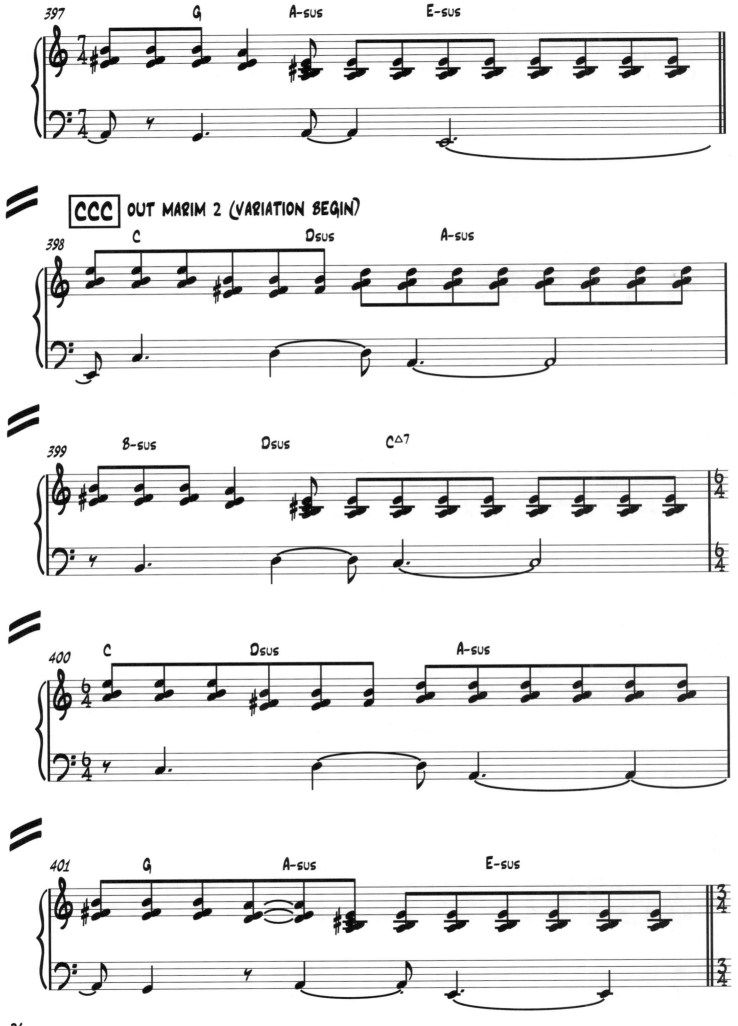

CCC OUT MARIM 2 (VARIATION BEGIN)

DDD REAL WRAP UP BEGINS

EEE KEY CHANGE

REPEATS

29

BASSLINE THEME END2

Rise Up
By Pat Metheny

34

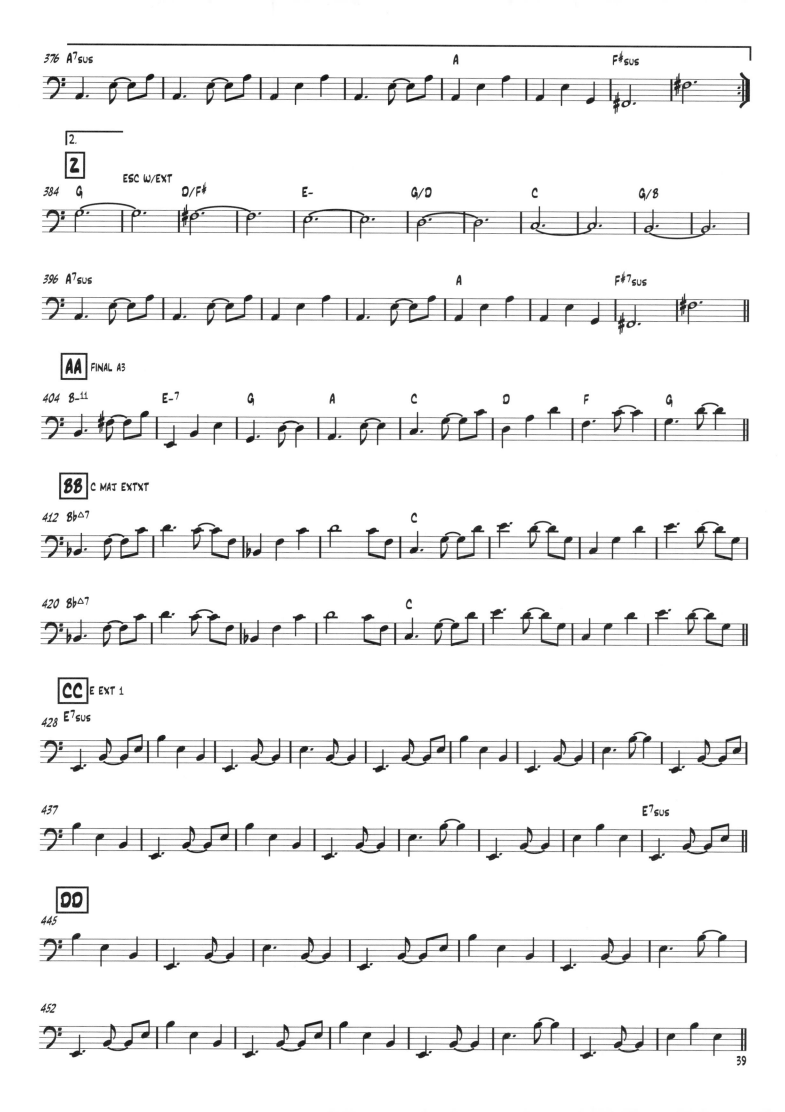

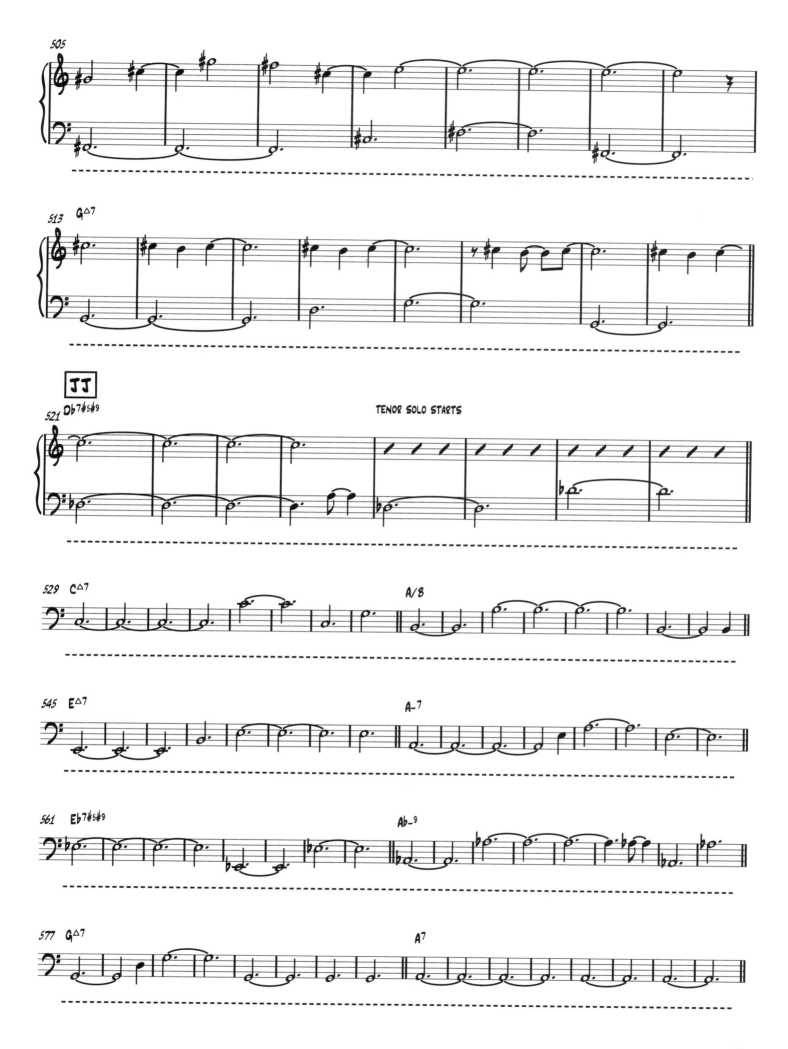

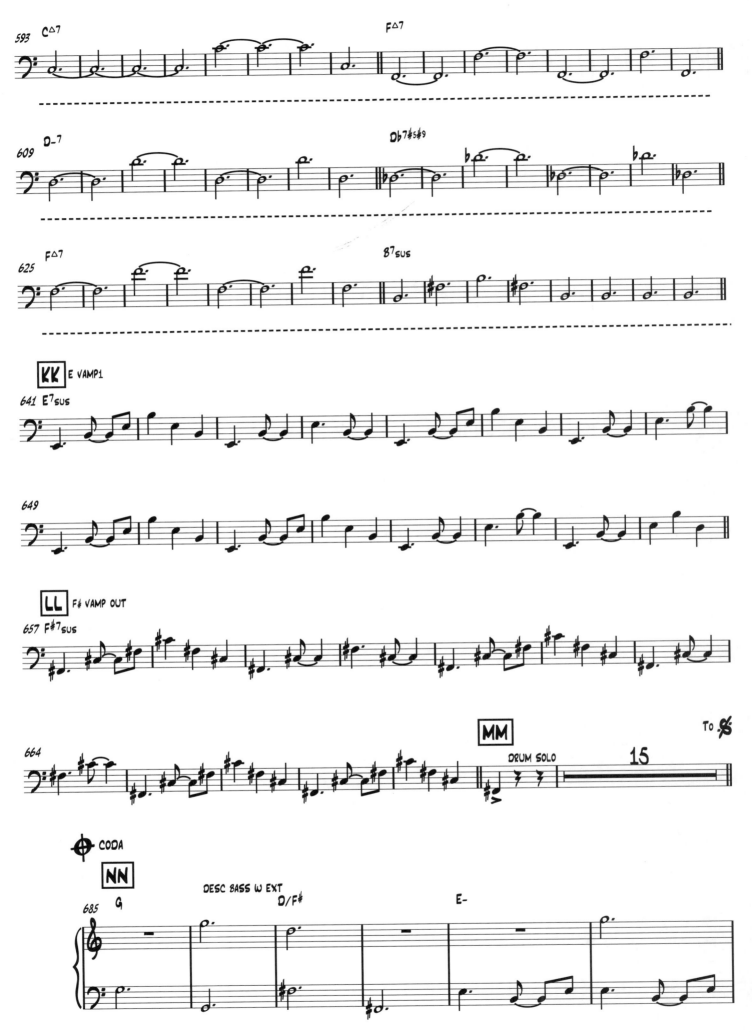

43

Adagia

By Pat Metheny

Sign of the Season

By Pat Metheny

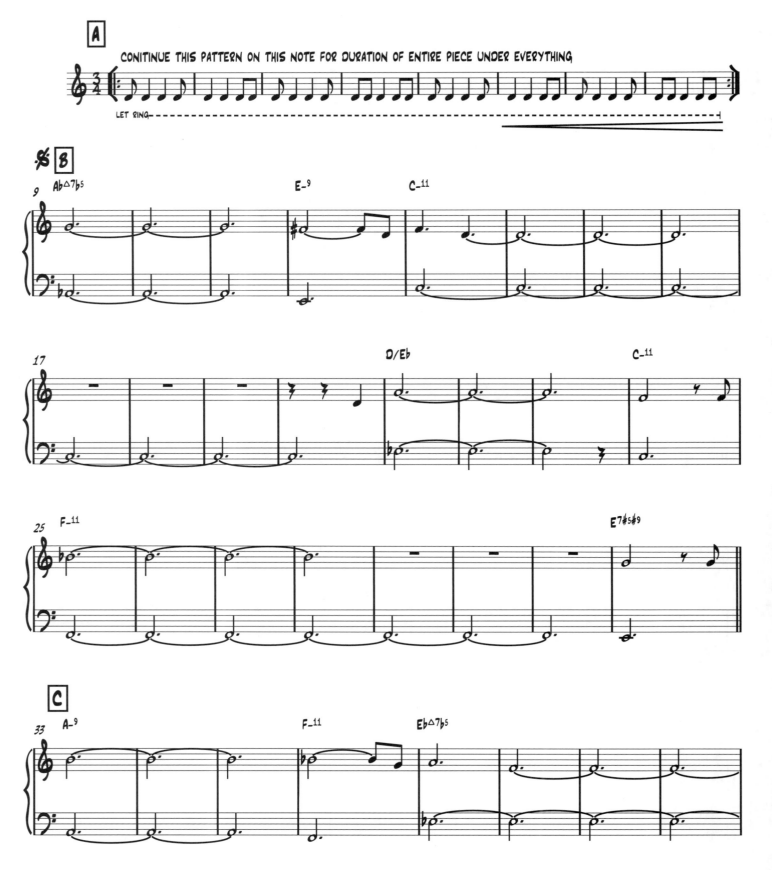

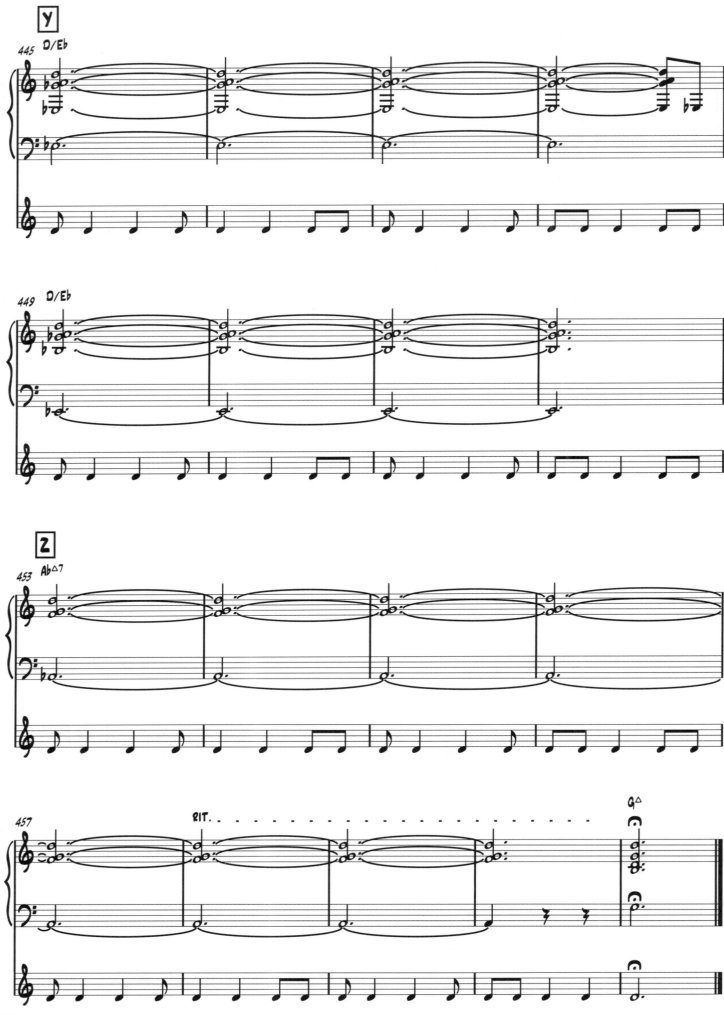

Kin
By Pat Metheny

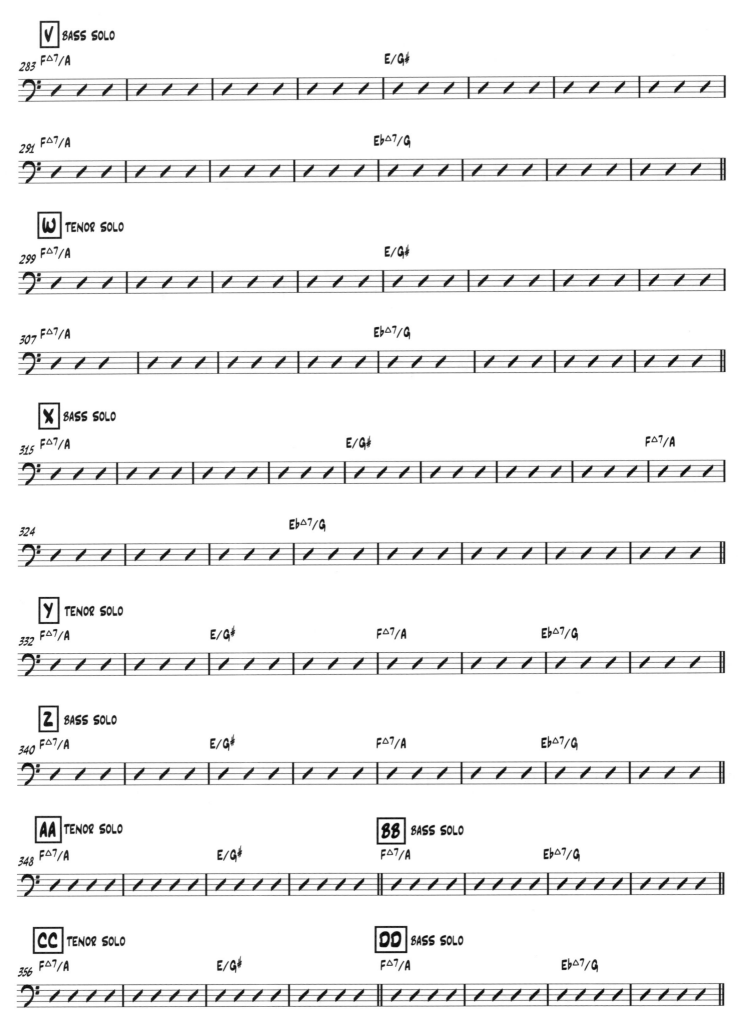

Born
By Pat Metheny

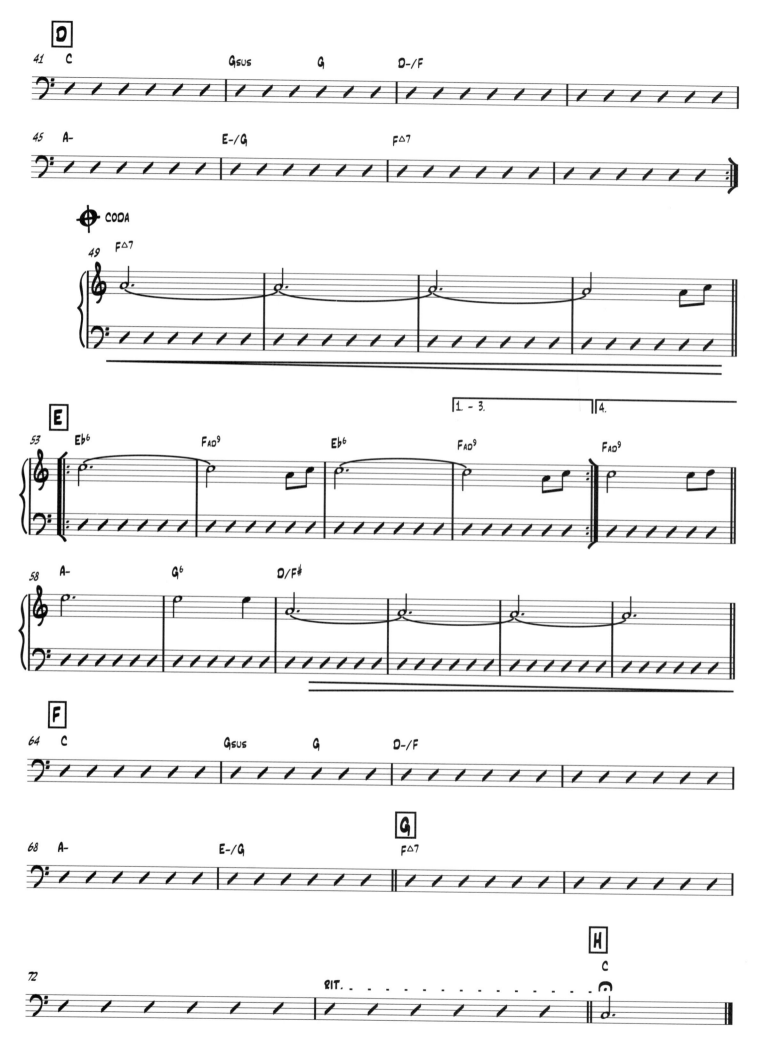

Genealogy
By Pat Metheny

Geneaolgy

By Pat Metheny

We Go On
By Pat Metheny

Kqu
By Pat Metheny

GUITAR RECORDED VERSIONS®

AUTHENTIC TRANSCRIPTIONS WITH NOTES AND TABLATURE

Guitar Recorded Versions® are note-for-note transcriptions of guitar music taken directly off recordings. This series, one of the most popular in print today, features some of the greatest guitar players and groups from blues and rock to country and jazz.

Guitar Recorded Versions are transcribed by the best transcribers in the business. Every book contains notes and tablature unless otherwise marked. Visit **www.halleonard.com** for our complete selection.

14041344 The Definitive AC/DC Songbook $45.99
00690016 The Will Ackerman Collection $22.99
00690501 Bryan Adams – Greatest Hits $22.99
00690603 Aerosmith – O Yeah! (Ultimate Hits) $24.95
00690178 Alice in Chains – Acoustic $19.99
00694865 Alice in Chains – Dirt $19.99
00660225 Alice in Chains – Facelift $19.95
00694925 Alice in Chains – Jar of Flies/Sap $19.99
00690387 Alice in Chains – Nothing Safe: Best of the Box $19.95
00694932 Allman Brothers Band – Definitive Collection for Guitar Volume 1 $24.95
00694933 Allman Brothers Band – Definitive Collection for Guitar Volume 2 $24.95
00694934 Allman Brothers Band – Definitive Collection for Guitar Volume 3 $24.99
00690958 Duane Allman Guitar Anthology $24.99
00691071 Alter Bridge – AB III $22.99
00690945 Alter Bridge – Blackbird $22.99
00690755 Alter Bridge – One Day Remains $22.99
00123558 Arctic Monkeys – AM $22.99
00114564 As I Lay Dying – Awakened $22.99
00690158 Chet Atkins – Almost Alone $19.95
00694876 Chet Atkins – Contemporary Styles $19.95
00694878 Chet Atkins – Vintage Fingerstyle $19.99
00690609 Audioslave $22.99
00690884 Audioslave – Revelations $19.95
00690926 Avenged Sevenfold $22.95
00214869 Avenged Sevenfold – The Best of 2005-2013 $24.99
00690820 Avenged Sevenfold – City of Evil $24.95
00123216 Avenged Sevenfold – Hail to the King $22.99
00222486 Avenged Sevenfold – The Stage $24.99
00691065 Avenged Sevenfold – Waking the Fallen $22.99
00123140 The Avett Brothers Guitar Collection $22.99
00694918 Randy Bachman Collection $22.95
00690503 Beach Boys – Very Best of $19.99
00694929 Beatles: 1962-1966 $24.99
00694930 Beatles: 1967-1970 $24.99
00690489 Beatles – 1 $24.99
00694880 Beatles – Abbey Road $19.95
00691066 Beatles – Beatles for Sale $22.99
00690110 Beatles – Book 1 (White Album) $19.99
00690111 Beatles – Book 2 (White Album) $19.95
00690902 Beatles – The Capitol Albums, Volume 1 $24.99
00694832 Beatles – For Acoustic Guitar $24.99
00691031 Beatles – Help! $19.99
00690482 Beatles – Let It Be $19.99
00691067 Beatles – Meet the Beatles! $22.99
00691068 Beatles – Please Please Me $22.99
00694891 Beatles – Revolver $19.95
00694914 Beatles – Rubber Soul $22.99
00694863 Beatles – Sgt. Pepper's Lonely Hearts Club Band $22.99
00110193 Beatles – Tomorrow Never Knows $22.99
00691044 Jeff Beck – Best of Beck $24.99
00690632 Beck – Sea Change $19.95
00691041 Jeff Beck – Truth $19.99
00694884 Best of George Benson $19.95
00692385 Chuck Berry $22.99
00690835 Billy Talent $19.95
00690879 Billy Talent II $19.99
00147787 Best of the Black Crowes $19.99
00129737 The Black Keys – Turn Blue $22.99
00690149 Black Sabbath $16.99
00690901 Best of Black Sabbath $19.95
00691010 Black Sabbath – Heaven and Hell $22.99
00690148 Black Sabbath – Master of Reality $16.99
00690142 Black Sabbath – Paranoid $16.99
14042759 Black Sabbath – 13 $19.99
00692200 Black Sabbath – We Sold Our Soul for Rock 'N' Roll $22.99
00690389 blink-182 – Enema of the State $19.95
00690831 blink-182 – Greatest Hits $19.95
00691179 blink-182 – Neighborhoods $22.99
00148544 Michael Bloomfield Guitar Anthology $24.99
00690028 Blue Oyster Cult – Cult Classics $19.99
00286622 Bohemian Rhapsody $24.99
00691074 Bon Jovi – Greatest Hits $22.99
00158600 Joe Bonamassa – Blues of Desperation $22.99
00139086 Joe Bonamassa – Different Shades of Blue $22.99
00198117 Joe Bonamassa – Muddy Wolf at Red Rocks $24.99
00283540 Joe Bonamassa – Redemption $24.99
00160988 Bootleg Country Guitar Tabs $19.99
00690913 Boston $19.95
00690829 Boston Guitar Collection $19.99
00690491 Best of David Bowie $19.99
00690583 Box Car Racer $19.95
00691023 Breaking Benjamin – Dear Agony $22.99
00690873 Breaking Benjamin – Phobia $19.95
00141446 Best of Lenny Breau $19.99
00690451 Jeff Buckley Collection $24.99
00690957 Bullet for My Valentine – Scream Aim Fire $22.99
00119629 Bullet for My Valentine – Temper Temper $22.99
00690678 Best of Kenny Burrell $19.99
00691077 Cage the Elephant – Thank You, Happy Birthday $22.99
00691159 The Cars – Complete Greatest Hits $22.99
00690261 Carter Family Collection $19.99
00691079 Best of Johnny Cash $22.99
00690043 Best of Cheap Trick $19.95
00690171 Chicago – The Definitive Guitar Collection $24.99
00691011 Chimaira Guitar Collection $24.99
00690567 Charlie Christian – The Definitive Collection $19.95
00101916 Eric Church – Chief $22.99
00129545 The Civil Wars $19.99
00138731 Eric Clapton & Friends – The Breeze $22.99
00690590 Eric Clapton – Anthology $29.95
00692391 Best of Eric Clapton – 2nd Edition $22.95
00691055 Eric Clapton – Clapton $22.99
00690936 Eric Clapton – Complete Clapton $29.99
00690010 Eric Clapton – From the Cradle $22.99
00192383 Eric Clapton – I Still Do* $19.99
00690363 Eric Clapton – Just One Night $24.99
00694873 Eric Clapton – Timepieces $19.95
00694869 Eric Clapton – Unplugged $22.95
00690415 Clapton Chronicles – Best of Eric Clapton $18.95
00694896 John Mayall/Eric Clapton – Bluesbreakers $19.99
00690162 Best of the Clash $19.99
00690828 Coheed & Cambria – Good Apollo I'm Burning Star, IV, Vol. 1: From Fear Through the Eyes of Madness $19.95
00690806 Coldplay – X & Y $19.95
00690855 Best of Collective Soul $19.95
00141704 Jesse Cook – Works Vol. 1 $19.99
00691091 The Best of Alice Cooper $22.99
00694940 Counting Crows – August & Everything After $19.99
00127184 Best of Robert Cray $19.99
00694840 Cream – Disraeli Gears $24.99
00690819 Best of Creedence Clearwater Revival $24.99
00690648 The Very Best of Jim Croce $19.99
00690572 Steve Cropper – Soul Man $19.99
00690613 Best of Crosby, Stills & Nash $27.99
00699521 The Cure – Greatest Hits $24.99
00690637 Best of Dick Dale $19.95
00690822 Best of Alex De Grassi $19.95
00690967 Death Cab for Cutie – Narrow Stairs $22.99
00690289 Best of Deep Purple $19.99
00690288 Deep Purple – Machine Head $17.99
00690784 Best of Def Leppard $22.99
00694831 Derek and the Dominos – Layla & Other Assorted Love Songs $22.95
00692240 Bo Diddley – Guitar Solos by Fred Sokolow $19.99
00690384 Best of Ani DiFranco $19.95
00690979 Best of Dinosaur Jr. $19.99
00690833 Private Investigations – Best of Dire Straits and Mark Knopfler $24.99
00695382 Very Best of Dire Straits – Sultans of Swing $24.99
00122443 Dream Theater $24.99
00160579 Dream Theater – Selections from The Astonishing $24.99
00278631 Eagles – Their Greatest Hits 1971-1975 $22.99
00278632 The Very Best of Eagles – Updated Edition $34.99
00690250 Best of Duane Eddy $17.99
00690909 Best of Tommy Emmanuel $24.99
00172824 Tommy Emmanuel – It's Never Too Late $22.99
00690555 Best of Melissa Etheridge $19.95
00690515 Extreme II – Pornograffitti $22.99
00150257 John Fahey – Guitar Anthology $19.99
00691009 Five Finger Death Punch $19.99
00690664 Best of Fleetwood Mac $22.99
00690870 Flyleaf $19.95
00691115 Foo Fighters – Wasting Light $22.99
00690805 Best of Robben Ford $22.99
00120220 Robben Ford – Guitar Anthology $24.99
00690842 Best of Peter Frampton $19.95
00694920 Best of Free $19.99
00694807 Danny Gatton – 88 Elmira St $22.99
00690438 Genesis Guitar Anthology $22.99
00690753 Best of Godsmack $19.95
00120167 Godsmack $19.95
00212480 Green Day – Revolution Radio* $19.99
00113073 Green Day – Uno $21.99
00116846 Green Day – ¡Dos! $21.99
00118259 Green Day – ¡Tré! $21.99
00691190 Best of Peter Green $19.99
00287515 Great Van Fleet – From the Fires $19.99
00690927 Patty Griffin – Children Running Through $19.95
00690591 Patty Griffin – Guitar Collection $19.95
00691027 Buddy Guy Anthology $24.99
00694854 Buddy Guy – Damn Right, I've Got the Blues $19.95
00690697 Best of Jim Hall $19.95
00690840 Ben Harper – Both Sides of the Gun $19.95
00691018 Ben Harper – Fight for Your Mind $22.99
00694798 George Harrison Anthology $22.99
00690841 Scott Henderson – Blues Guitar Collection $22.99
00692930 Jimi Hendrix – Are You Experienced? $24.95
00692931 Jimi Hendrix – Axis: Bold As Love $22.95
00690304 Jimi Hendrix – Band of Gypsys $24.99
00690608 Jimi Hendrix – Blue Wild Angel $24.95
00694944 Jimi Hendrix – Blues $24.99
00275044 Jimi Hendrix – Both Sides of the Sky $22.99
00692932 Jimi Hendrix – Electric Ladyland $24.95
00119619 Jimi Hendrix – People, Hell and Angels $22.99
00690602 Jimi Hendrix – Smash Hits $24.99
00691152 West Coast Seattle Boy: The Jimi Hendrix Anthology $29.99
00691332 Jimi Hendrix – Winterland (Highlights) $22.99
00690017 Jimi Hendrix – Woodstock $29.99
00690843 H.I.M. – Dark Light $19.95
00690869 Hinder – Extreme Behavior $19.95
00660029 Buddy Holly $22.99
00690793 John Lee Hooker Anthology $24.99
00694905 Howlin' Wolf $19.95
00690692 Very Best of Billy Idol $22.99
00121961 Imagine Dragons – Night Visions $22.99
00690688 Incubus – A Crow Left of the Murder $19.95
00690790 Iron Maiden Anthology $24.99
00691058 Iron Maiden – The Final Frontier $22.99
00200446 Iron Maiden – Guitar Tab $29.99
00690887 Iron Maiden – A Matter of Life and Death $24.95
00690730 Alan Jackson – Guitar Collection $22.99
00694938 Elmore James – Master Electric Slide Guitar $19.99
00690652 Best of Jane's Addiction $19.95
00690684 Jethro Tull – Aqualung $19.99
00690693 Jethro Tull Guitar Anthology $22.99

00691182	Jethro Tull – Stand Up	$22.99
00690898	John 5 – The Devil Knows My Name	$22.95
00690814	John 5 – Songs for Sanity	$19.95
00690751	John 5 – Vertigo	$19.95
00694912	Eric Johnson – Ah Via Musicom	$22.99
00690660	Best of Eric Johnson	$22.99
00691076	Eric Johnson – Up Close	$22.99
00690169	Eric Johnson – Venus Isle	$22.95
00122439	Jack Johnson – From Here to Now to You	$22.99
00690846	Jack Johnson and Friends – Sing-A-Longs and Lullabies for the Film Curious George	$19.95
00690271	Robert Johnson – The New Transcriptions	$24.99
00699131	Best of Janis Joplin	$19.95
00690427	Best of Judas Priest	$24.99
00690277	Best of Kansas	$19.99
00690911	Best of Phil Keaggy	$24.99
00690727	Toby Keith Guitar Collection	$19.99
00120814	Killswitch Engage – Disarm the Descent	$22.99
00690504	Very Best of Albert King	$19.95
00124869	Albert King with Stevie Ray Vaughan – In Session	$22.99
00130447	B.B. King – Live at the Regal	$17.99
00690444	B.B. King & Eric Clapton – Riding with the King	$24.99
00690134	Freddie King Collection	$19.95
00691062	Kings of Leon – Come Around Sundown	$22.99
00690157	Kiss – Alive!	$19.95
00690356	Kiss – Alive II	$22.99
00694903	Best of Kiss for Guitar	$24.99
00690355	Kiss – Destroyer	$16.95
00690164	Mark Knopfler Guitar – Vol. 1	$24.99
00690163	Mark Knopfler/Chet Atkins – Neck and Neck	$22.99
00690780	Korn – Greatest Hits, Volume 1	$22.95
00690377	Kris Kristofferson Collection	$19.99
00690834	Lamb of God – Ashes of the Wake	$19.95
00690875	Lamb of God – Sacrament	$22.99
00690977	Ray LaMontagne – Gossip in the Grain	$19.99
00691057	Ray LaMontagne and the Pariah Dogs – God Willin' & The Creek Don't Rise	$22.99
00690922	Linkin Park – Minutes to Midnight	$19.99
00114563	The Lumineers	$22.99
00690525	Best of George Lynch	$24.99
00690955	Lynyrd Skynyrd – All-Time Greatest Hits	$22.99
00694954	New Best of Lynyrd Skynyrd	$22.99
00690577	Yngwie Malmsteen – Anthology	$27.99
00209846	Mammoth Metal Guitar Tab Anthology	$29.99
00690754	Marilyn Manson – Lest We Forget	$19.99
00694956	Bob Marley – Legend	$19.95
00690548	Very Best of Bob Marley & The Wailers – One Love	$22.99
00694945	Bob Marley – Songs of Freedom	$24.95
00690657	Maroon 5 – Songs About Jane	$19.95
00690989	Mastodon – Crack the Skye	$24.99
00236690	Mastodon – Emperor of Sand	$22.99
00119220	Brent Mason – Hot Wired	$19.99
00236690	Mastodon – Emperor of Sand	$22.99
00691176	Mastodon – The Hunter	$22.99
00137718	Mastodon – Once More 'Round the Sun	$22.99
00691942	Andy McKee – Art of Motion	$22.99
00691034	Andy McKee – Joyland	$19.99
00120080	The Don McLean Songbook	$19.99
00694952	Megadeth – Countdown to Extinction	$24.99
00690244	Megadeth – Cryptic Writings	$19.95
00276065	Megadeth – Greatest Hits: Back to the Start	$24.99
00694951	Megadeth – Rust in Peace	$24.99
00690011	Megadeth – Youthanasia	$22.99
00690505	John Mellencamp Guitar Collection	$19.99
00209876	Metallica – Hardwired... To Self-Destruct	$22.99
00690562	Pat Metheny – Bright Size Life	$19.95
00691073	Pat Metheny with Christian McBride & Antonion Sanchez – Day Trip/Tokyo Day Trip Live	$22.99
00690646	Pat Metheny – One Quiet Night	$19.95
00690559	Pat Metheny – Question & Answer	$22.99
00118836	Pat Metheny – Unity Band	$22.99
00102590	Pat Metheny – What's It All About	$22.99
00690040	Steve Miller Band Greatest Hits	$19.99
00119338	Ministry Guitar Tab Collection	$24.99
00102591	Wes Montgomery Guitar Anthology	$24.99
00694802	Gary Moore – Still Got the Blues	$22.99
00691005	Best of Motion City Soundtrack	$19.99
00129884	Jason Mraz – Yes!	$22.99
00691070	Mumford & Sons – Sigh No More	$22.99
00118196	Muse – The 2nd Law	$19.99
00690996	My Morning Jacket Collection	$19.99
00690984	Matt Nathanson – Some Mad Hope	$22.99
00690611	Nirvana	$22.95
00694895	Nirvana – Bleach	$19.99
00694913	Nirvana – In Utero	$19.99
00694883	Nirvana – Nevermind	$19.99
00690026	Nirvana – Unplugged in New York	$19.99
00265439	Nothing More – Guitar & Bass Tab Collection	$24.99
00307163	Oasis – Time Flies... 1994-2009	$24.99
00243349	The Best of Opeth	$22.99
00691052	Roy Orbison – Black & White Night	$22.99
00694847	Best of Ozzy Osbourne	$24.99
00690933	Best of Brad Paisley	$24.99
00690995	Brad Paisley – Play: The Guitar Album	$24.99
00690939	Christopher Parkening – Solo Pieces	$19.99
00690594	Best of Les Paul	$19.95
00694855	Pearl Jam – Ten	$22.99
00690439	A Perfect Circle – Mer De Noms	$19.99
00690725	Best of Carl Perkins	$19.99
00690499	Tom Petty – Definitive Guitar Collection	$19.99
00690176	Phish – Billy Breathes	$22.95
00121933	Pink Floyd – Acoustic Guitar Collection	$24.99
00690428	Pink Floyd – Dark Side of the Moon	$19.95
00239799	Pink Floyd – The Wall	$24.99
00690789	Best of Poison	$19.99
00690299	Best of Elvis: The King of Rock 'n' Roll	$19.99
00692535	Elvis Presley	$19.95
00690925	The Very Best of Prince	$22.99
00690003	Classic Queen	$24.95
00694975	Queen – Greatest Hits	$25.99
00254332	Queens of the Stone Age – Villains	$22.99
00690670	Very Best of Queensryche	$24.99
00690878	The Raconteurs – Broken Boy Soldiers	$19.95
00109303	Radiohead Guitar Anthology	$24.99
00694910	Rage Against the Machine	$22.99
00119834	Rage Against the Machine – Guitar Anthology	$22.99
00690179	Rancid – And Out Come the Wolves	$24.99
00690426	Best of Ratt	$19.95
00690055	Red Hot Chili Peppers – Blood Sugar Sex Magik	$19.99
00690584	Red Hot Chili Peppers – By the Way	$22.99
00690379	Red Hot Chili Peppers – Californication	$19.99
00690673	Red Hot Chili Peppers – Greatest Hits	$19.99
00690090	Red Hot Chili Peppers – One Hot Minute	$22.95
00691166	Red Hot Chili Peppers – I'm with You	$22.99
00690852	Red Hot Chili Peppers – Stadium Arcadium	$27.99
00690511	Django Reinhardt – The Definitive Collection	$22.99
00690643	Relient K – Two Lefts Don't Make a Right ... But Three Do	$19.95
00690260	Jimmie Rodgers Guitar Collection	$22.99
14041901	Rodrigo Y Gabriela and C.U.B.A. – Area 52	$24.99
00690014	Rolling Stones – Exile on Main Street	$24.95
00690631	Rolling Stones – Guitar Anthology	$29.99
00690685	David Lee Roth – Eat 'Em and Smile	$22.99
00174797	Santana – IV*	$22.99
00173534	Santana Guitar Anthology	$24.99
00690031	Santana's Greatest Hits	$19.95
00276350	Joe Satriani – What Happens Next	$24.99
00690796	Very Best of Michael Schenker	$19.95
00128870	Matt Schofield Guitar Tab Collection	$22.99
00690566	Best of Scorpions	$24.99
00690604	Bob Seger – Guitar Anthology	$22.99
00234543	Ed Sheeran – Divide	$19.99
00138870	Ed Sheeran – X	$19.99
00690803	Best of Kenny Wayne Shepherd Band	$19.95
00122218	Skillet – Rise	$22.99
00691114	Slash – Guitar Anthology	$27.99
00690872	Slayer – Christ Illusion	$19.95
00690813	Slayer – Guitar Collection	$19.99
00690419	Slipknot	$19.95
00690973	Slipknot – All Hope Is Gone	$22.99
00690330	Social Distortion – Live at the Roxy	$19.95
00120004	Best of Steely Dan	$24.99
00694921	Best of Steppenwolf	$22.95
00690655	Best of Mike Stern	$24.99
14041588	Cat Stevens – Tea for the Tillerman	$19.99
00690949	Rod Stewart Guitar Anthology	$19.99
00690021	Sting – Fields of Gold	$19.95
00690520	Styx Guitar Collection	$19.95
00120081	Sublime	$19.99
00690992	Sublime – Robbin' the Hood	$19.99
00690519	SUM 41 – All Killer No Filler	$19.95
00691072	Best of Supertramp	$22.99
00142151	Taylor Swift – 1989	$22.99
00115957	Taylor Swift – Red	$21.99
00691063	Taylor Swift – Speak Now	$22.99
00690767	Switchfoot – The Beautiful Letdown	$19.95
00690531	System of a Down – Toxicity	$19.99
00694824	Best of James Taylor	$19.99
00694887	Best of Thin Lizzy	$19.95
00690891	30 Seconds to Mars – A Beautiful Lie	$19.95
00690233	The Merle Travis Collection	$22.99
00253237	Trivium – Guitar Tab Anthology	$24.99
00690683	Robin Trower – Bridge of Sighs	$19.99
00699191	U2 – Best of: 1980-1990	$19.99
00690732	U2 – Best of: 1990-2000	$19.95
00690894	U2 – 18 Singles	$22.99
00124461	Keith Urban – Guitar Anthology	$19.99
00690039	Steve Vai – Alien Love Secrets	$24.95
00690172	Steve Vai – Fire Garden	$24.95
00197570	Steve Vai – Modern Primitive	$29.99
00690881	Steve Vai – Real Illusions: Reflections	$24.95
00694904	Steve Vai – Sex and Religion	$24.95
00110385	Steve Vai – The Story of Light	$22.99
00690392	Steve Vai – The Ultra Zone	$19.95
00700555	Van Halen – Van Halen	$19.99
00690024	Stevie Ray Vaughan – Couldn't Stand the Weather	$19.99
00690116	Stevie Ray Vaughan – Guitar Collection	$24.95
00694879	Stevie Ray Vaughan – In the Beginning	$19.95
00660058	Stevie Ray Vaughan – Lightnin' Blues '83-'87	$27.99
00217455	Stevie Ray Vaughan – Plays Slow Blues	$19.99
00694835	Stevie Ray Vaughan – The Sky Is Crying	$22.95
00690025	Stevie Ray Vaughan – Soul to Soul	$19.95
00690015	Stevie Ray Vaughan – Texas Flood	$19.99
00109770	Volbeat Guitar Collection	$22.99
00121808	Volbeat – Outlaw Gentlemen & Shady Ladies	$22.99
00183213	Volbeat – Seal the Deal & Let's Boogie*	$19.99
00690132	The T-Bone Walker Collection	$19.99
00150209	Trans-Siberian Orchestra Guitar Anthology	$19.99
00694789	Muddy Waters – Deep Blues	$24.99
00152161	Doc Watson – Guitar Anthology	$22.99
00690071	Weezer (The Blue Album)	$19.95
00691046	Weezer – Rarities Edition	$22.99
00172118	Weezer (The White Album)*	$19.99
00117511	Whitesnake Guitar Collection	$19.99
00690447	Best of the Who	$24.95
00691941	The Who – Acoustic Guitar Collection	$22.99
00691006	Wilco Guitar Collection	$22.99
00691017	Wolfmother – Cosmic Egg	$22.99
00690319	Stevie Wonder – Hits	$19.99
00690596	Best of the Yardbirds	$19.99
00690916	The Best of Dwight Yoakam	$19.95
00691020	Neil Young – After the Goldrush	$22.99
00691019	Neil Young – Everybody Knows This Is Nowhere	$19.99
00690904	Neil Young – Harvest	$29.99
00691021	Neil Young – Harvest Moon	$22.99
00690905	Neil Young – Rust Never Sleeps	$19.99
00690443	Frank Zappa – Hot Rats	$19.99
00690624	Frank Zappa and the Mothers of Invention – One Size Fits All	$22.99
00690623	Frank Zappa – Over-Nite Sensation	$22.99
00121684	ZZ Top – Early Classics	$24.99
00690589	ZZ Top – Guitar Anthology	$24.99
00690960	ZZ Top Guitar Classics	$19.99

RECORDED VERSIONS GUITAR®

AUTHENTIC TRANSCRIPTIONS WITH NOTES AND TABLATURE

HAL•LEONARD®

*Tab transcriptions only.

Complete songlists and more at **www.halleonard.com**

Prices, contents, and availability subject to change without notice.

0319
149

GUITAR *signature licks*®

Signature Licks book/audio packs provide a step-by-step breakdown of "right from the record" riffs, licks, and solos so you can jam along with your favorite bands. They contain performance notes and an overview of each artist's or group's style, with note-for-note transcriptions in notes and tab. The CDs or online audio tracks feature full-band demos at both normal and slow speeds.

AC/DC
14041352.................................. $22.99

AEROSMITH 1973-1979
00695106 .... $22.95

AEROSMITH 1979-1998
00695219 .... $22.95

DUANE ALLMAN
00696042 .... $22.99

BEST OF CHET ATKINS
00695752.................................$24.99

AVENGED SEVENFOLD
00696473 .... $22.99

BEST OF THE BEATLES FOR ACOUSTIC GUITAR
00695453 .... $22.99

THE BEATLES BASS
00695283 .... $22.99

THE BEATLES FAVORITES
00695096.................................$24.95

THE BEATLES HITS
00695049.................................$24.95

JEFF BECK
00696427 .... $22.99

BEST OF GEORGE BENSON
00695418 .... $22.99

BEST OF BLACK SABBATH
00695249 .... $22.95

BLUES BREAKERS WITH JOHN MAYALL & ERIC CLAPTON
00696374 .... $22.99

BON JOVI
00696380 .... $22.99

ROY BUCHANAN
00696654 .... $22.99

KENNY BURRELL
00695830.................................$24.99

BEST OF CHARLIE CHRISTIAN
00695584 .... $22.95

BEST OF ERIC CLAPTON
00695038.................................$24.99

ERIC CLAPTON – FROM THE ALBUM UNPLUGGED
00695250.................................$24.95

BEST OF CREAM
00695251 .... $22.95

CREEDANCE CLEARWATER REVIVAL
00695924................................. $22.95

DEEP PURPLE – GREATEST HITS
00695625 .... $22.99

THE BEST OF DEF LEPPARD
00696516 .... $22.99

DREAM THEATER
00111943 ....$24.99

TOMMY EMMANUEL
00696409 .... $22.99

ESSENTIAL JAZZ GUITAR
00695875 .... $19.99

FAMOUS ROCK GUITAR SOLOS
00695590 .... $19.95

FLEETWOOD MAC
00696416 .... $22.99

BEST OF FOO FIGHTERS
00695481 .... $24.95

ROBBEN FORD
00695903 .... $22.95

BEST OF GRANT GREEN
00695747 .... $22.99

PETER GREEN
00145386 .... $22.99

THE GUITARS OF ELVIS – 2ND ED.
00174800 .... $22.99

BEST OF GUNS N' ROSES
00695183 ....$24.99

THE BEST OF BUDDY GUY
00695186 .... $22.99

JIM HALL
00695848 ....$24.99

JIMI HENDRIX
00696560.................................$24.99

JIMI HENDRIX – VOLUME 2
00695835 ....$24.99

JOHN LEE HOOKER
00695894.................................$19.99

BEST OF JAZZ GUITAR
00695586 .... $24.95

ERIC JOHNSON
00699317.................................$24.99

ROBERT JOHNSON
00695264 .... $22.95

BARNEY KESSEL
00696009.................................$24.99

THE ESSENTIAL ALBERT KING
00695713................................. $22.95

B.B. KING – BLUES LEGEND
00696039 .... $22.99

B.B. KING – THE DEFINITIVE COLLECTION
00695635................................. $22.95

B.B. KING – MASTER BLUESMAN
00699923.................................$24.99

MARK KNOPFLER
00695178.................................$24.99

LYNYRD SKYNYRD
00695872.................................$24.99

THE BEST OF YNGWIE MALMSTEEN
00695669 .... $22.95

BEST OF PAT MARTINO
00695632.................................$24.99

MEGADETH
00696421 .... $22.99

WES MONTGOMERY
00695387.................................$24.99

BEST OF NIRVANA
00695483.................................$24.95

VERY BEST OF OZZY OSBOURNE
00695431 .... $22.99

BRAD PAISLEY
00696379 .... $22.99

BEST OF JOE PASS
00695730 .... $22.99

JACO PASTORIUS
00695544.................................$24.95

TOM PETTY
00696021 .... $22.99

PINK FLOYD
00103659.................................$24.99

BEST OF QUEEN
00695097.................................$24.99

RADIOHEAD
00109304.................................$24.99

BEST OF RAGE AGAINST THE MACHINE
00695480.................................$24.95

RED HOT CHILI PEPPERS
00695173 .... $22.95

RED HOT CHILI PEPPERS – GREATEST HITS
00695828.................................$24.99

JERRY REED
00118236 .... $22.99

BEST OF DJANGO REINHARDT
00695660.................................$24.99

BEST OF ROCK 'N' ROLL GUITAR
00695559 .... $22.99

BEST OF ROCKABILLY GUITAR
00695785 .... $19.95

BEST OF CARLOS SANTANA
00174664 .... $22.99

BEST OF JOE SATRIANI
00695216 .... $22.95

SLASH
00696576.................................. $22.99

SLAYER
00121281.................................. $22.99

THE BEST OF SOUL GUITAR
00695703.................................$19.95

BEST OF SOUTHERN ROCK
00695560.................................$19.95

STEELY DAN
00696015 .... $22.99

MIKE STERN
00695800.................................$24.99

BEST OF SURF GUITAR
00695822.................................$19.99

STEVE VAI
00673247 .... $22.95

STEVE VAI – ALIEN LOVE SECRETS: THE NAKED VAMPS
00695223.................................$22.95

STEVE VAI – FIRE GARDEN: THE NAKED VAMPS
00695166 .... $22.95

STEVE VAI – THE ULTRA ZONE: NAKED VAMPS
00695684.................................$22.95

VAN HALEN
00110227.................................$24.99

STEVIE RAY VAUGHAN – 2ND ED.
00699316.................................$24.95

THE GUITAR STYLE OF STEVIE RAY VAUGHAN
00695155 ....$24.95

BEST OF THE VENTURES
00695772.................................$19.95

THE WHO – 2ND ED.
00695561 .... $22.95

JOHNNY WINTER
00695951 .... $22.99

YES
00113120.................................$22.99

NEIL YOUNG – GREATEST HITS
00695988 .... $22.99

BEST OF ZZ TOP
00695738.................................$24.95

HAL•LEONARD®

www.halleonard.com

COMPLETE DESCRIPTIONS AND SONGLISTS ONLINE!
Prices, contents and availability subject to change without notice.